GUIDE

TO

THE PRINCIPAL PICTURES

IN THE

ACADEMY OF FINE ARTS

AT

VENICE.

ARRANGED FOR ENGLISH TRAVELLERS

BY

JOHN RUSKIN,

SLADE PROFESSOR OF FINE ART, OXFORD, AND HONORARY ASSOCIATE OF THE ACADEMY OF VENICE.

VENICE, MDCCCLXXVII.

GUIDE, ETC.

In the first place, if the weather is fine, go outside the gate you have just come in at, and look above it. Over this door are three of the most precious pieces of sculpture in Venice; her native work, dated; and belonging to the school of severe Gothic which indicates the beginning of her Christian life in understanding of its real claims upon her.

St. Leonard on the left, St. Christopher on the right, under Gothic cusped niches. The Madonna in the centre, under a simple gable; the piece of sculpture itself engaged in a rectangular panel, which is the persistent sign of the Greek schools; descending from the Metopes of the Parthenon.

You see the infant sprawls on her knee in an ungainly manner:—she herself sits with quiet maiden dignity, but in no manner of sentimental adoration.

That is Venetian naturalism; showing their henceforward steady desire to represent things as they
really (according to the workman's notions) might
have existed. It begins first in this century sepa-
rating itself from the Byzantine formalism,—the
movement being the same which was led by Giotto
in Florence fifty years earlier. These sculptures
are the result of his influence, from Padua, and
other such Gothic power, rousing Venice to do
and think for herself, instead of letting her Greek
subjects do all for her. This is one of her first
performances, independently of them. She has not
yet the least notion of making anybody stand rightly
on their feet; you see how St. Leonard and St.
Christopher point their toes. Clearly, until we
know how to do better than this, in perspective and
such matters, our painting cannot come to much.
Accordingly, all the Venetian painting of any
importance you are now to see in the Academy
is subsequent to these sculptures. But these are,
fortunately, dated—1378 and 1379. Twenty years
more will bring us out of the fourteenth century.
And therefore, broadly, all the painter's art of Venice
begins in the fifteenth; and we may as well at once
take note that it ends with the sixteenth. There are
only these two hundred years of painting in Venice.
Now, without much pause in the corridor, though
the old well in the cortile has its notabilities if

one had time,—up the spiral stairs, and when you
have entered the gallery and got your admission
tickets—(quite a proper arrangement that you should
pay for them,—if *I* were a Venetian prefect, you
should pay a good deal more for leave to come to
Venice at all, that I might be sure you cared to
come,)—walk straight forward till you descend the
steps into the first room in the arrangement of
the Academy Catalogue. On your right, at the
bottom of the steps, you see a large picture (16)
in a series of compartments, of which the central
one, the Crowning of the Virgin, was painted by
a Venetian vicar, (vicar of St. Agnes,) in 1380.
A happy, faithful, cheerful vicar he must have
been; and any vicar, rector, or bishop who could
do such a thing now, would be a blessing to his
parish, and delight to his diocese. Symmetrical,
orderly, gay, and in the heart of it nobly grave,
this work of the old Plebanus has much in it of
the future methods of Venetian composition. The
two angels peeping over the arms of the throne may
remind you to look at its cusped arches, for we are
here in central Gothic time; thirty years after the
sea-façade of the Ducal Palace had been built.

Now, on the opposite side of the room, over the
door leading into the next room, you see (1) in
the Academy Catalogue "The work of Bartholomew
Vivarini of Murano, 1464," showing you what ad-

vance had been made in eighty years. The figures still hard in outline,—thin, (except the Madonna's throat, which always, in Venice, is strong as a pillar,) and much marked in sinew and bone, (studied from life, mind you, not by dissection); exquisitely delicate and careful in pure colour;—in character, portraits of holy men and women, such as then were. There is no idealism here whatever. Monks and nuns had indeed faces and mien like these saints, when they desired to have the saints painted for them.

A noble picture; not of any supreme genius, but completely containing the essence of Venetian art.

Next, going under it, through the door, you find yourself in the principal room of the Academy, which please cross quietly to the window opposite, on the left of which hangs a large picture which you will have great difficulty in seeing at all, hung as it is against the light; and which, in any of its finer qualities, you absolutely cannot see; but may yet perceive what they are, latent in that darkness, which is all the honour that the kings, nobles, and artists of Europe care to bestow on one of the greatest pictures ever painted by Christendom in her central art-power. Alone worth an entire modern exhibition-building, hired fiddlers, and all; here you have it jammed on a back wall, utterly unserviceable to human kind, the little angels of it fiddling unseen,

unheard by anybody's heart. It is the best John
Bellini in the Academy of Venice; the third best
in Venice, and probably in the world. Repainted,
the right-hand angel, and somewhat elsewhere; but
on the whole perfect; unspeakably good, and right
in all ways. Not inspired with any high religious
passion; a good man's work, not an enthusiast's. It
is, in principle, merely the perfecting of Vivarini's;
the saints, mere portraits of existing men and women;
the Madonna, idealized only in that squareness of
face and throat, not in anywise the prettier for it,
otherwise a quite commonplace Venetian woman.
Such, and far lovelier, you may see living to-day, if
you can see—and may make manifest, if you can
paint.

And now, you may look to the far end of the
room, where Titian's 'Assumption' has the chairs
put before it; everybody being expected to sit down,
and for once, without asking what o'clock it is at
the railroad station, reposefully admire.

Of which, hear first what I wrote, very rightly,
a quarter of a century ago.

"The traveller is generally too much struck by
Titian's great picture of 'The Assumption' to be
able to pay proper attention to the other works
in this gallery. Let him, however, ask himself
candidly how much of his admiration is dependent
merely on the picture's being larger than any other

in the room, and having bright masses of red and blue in it; let him be assured that the picture is in reality not one whit the better either for being large or gaudy in colour, and he will then be better disposed to give the pains necessary to discover the merit of the more profound works of Bellini and Tintoret."

I wrote this, I have said, *very* rightly, not *quite* rightly. For if a picture is good, it *is* better for being large, because it is more difficult to paint large than small; and if colour is good, it *may be* better for being bright.

Nay, the fault of this picture, as I read it now, is in not being bright enough. A large piece of scarlet, two large pieces of crimson, and some very beautiful blue, occupy about a fifth part of it; but the rest is mostly fox colour or dark brown: majority of the apostles under total eclipse of brown. St. John, there being nobody else handsome to look at, is therefore seen to advantage; also St. Peter and his beard; but the rest of the lower canvas is filled with little more than flourishings of arms and flingings of cloaks, in shadow and light.

However, as a piece of oil painting, and what artists call 'composition,' with entire grasp and knowledge of the action of the human body, the perspectives of the human face, and the relations of shade to colour in expressing form, the picture is deservedly held unsurpassable. Enjoy of it what you can; but of its place in the history of Venetian art observe these three following points :—

I. The throned Madonnas of Vivarini and Bellini were to Venice what the statue of Athena in the Brazen House was to Athens. Not at all supposed to *be* Athena, or to *be* Madonnas; but symbols, by help of which they conceived the presence with them of a real Goddess. But this picture of Titian's does not profess to symbolize any Virgin here with us; but only to show how the Virgin was taken away from us a long time ago. And professing to represent this, he does not in the least believe his own representation, nor expect anybody else to believe it. He does not, in his heart, believe the Assumption ever took place at all. He is merely putting together a stage decoration of clouds, little boys, with wings stuck into them, and pantomime actors, in studied positions, to amuse his Venice and himself.

II. Though desirous of nothing but amusement, he is not, at heart, half so much amused by his work as John Bellini, or the quarter so much amused as the innocent old vicar. On the contrary, a strange gloom has been cast over him, he knows not why; but he likes all his colours dark, and puts great spaces of brown, and crimson passing into black, where the older painters would have made all lively. ¡Painters call this ' chiaros-curo.' So also they may call a thunder-cloud in the sky of spring: but it means more than light and shade.

III. You see that in all the three earlier pictures everybody is quiet. Here, everybody is in a bustle. If you like to look at my pamphlet on the relation of Tintoret to Michael Angelo, you will see how this comes to pass, and what it means. And that is all I care for your noticing in the Assumption, just now.

Next, look on right and left of it at the two dark pictures over the doors (63, 25).

Darkness visible, with flashes of lightning through it. The thunder-cloud upon us, rent with fire.

Those are Tintorets; finest possible Tintorets; best possible examples of what, in absolute power of painting, is supremest work, so far as I know, in all the world.

Nothing comes near Tintoret for colossal painter's power, as such. But you need not think to get any good of these pictures: it would take you twenty years' work to understand the fineness of them as painting; and for the rest, there is little good in them to be got. Adam and Eve no more sat in that warm-weather picnic manner, helping each other politely to apples, on the occasion of their fall, than the Madonna went up all bending about in her red and blue cloak on the occasion of her Assumption. But of the wrong, and the truth, the error, and the glory of these pictures, I have no time to speak now; nor you to hear. All that you have to notice is that painting has now become a dark instead of bright art, and in many ways a frightful and unpleasant art, or else I will add once for all, referring you for proof of it to the general examples of Venetian work at this late epoch, supplied as a luxury to foreign courts, a lascivious art.*

Nevertheless up to the time when Tintoret painted the Crucifixion in the Scuola di San Rocco, Venice had not in heart abjured her religion. The time when the last chord of its faith gives way cannot be discerned, to day and hour; but in that day and hour of which, for external sign, we may best take the death of Tintoret in 1594, the Arts of Venice are at an end.

I have therefore now shown you the complete course of their power, from 1380 at the Academy

* One copy of Titian's work bearing such commercial value, and showing what was briefly the Gospel preached by Missionary Venice to foreign nations in the sixteenth century, you will find presently in the narrow corridor, No. 347: on which you will usually also find some modern copyist employed, for missionary purposes; but never on a Vivarini. And in thus becoming dark, terrific, and sensual, Venetian art led the way to the mere naturalism and various baseness of following European art with the rubbish of which that corridor (Sala ix., Numbers 276 to 358,) is mostly filled.

gates, to 1594—say, broadly, two centuries, (her previous art being only architectural, mosaic, or decorative sculpture). We will now go through the rooms, noticing what is best worth notice, in each of the epochs defined; essentially, you observe, three. The first we may call the Vivarini epoch, bright, innocent, more or less elementary, entirely religious art,—reaching from 1400 to 1480; the second, (which for reasons presently to .be shown, we will call the Carpaccian epoch,) sometimes classic and mythic as well as religious, 1480—1520; the third, supremely powerful art corrupted by taint of death, 1520—1600, which we will call the Tintoret epoch.

Of course the lives of the painters run in and out across these limits ; yet if you fasten these firmly in your mind,—80, 40, 80,—you will find you have an immense advantage and easy grip of the whole history of Venetian art.

In the first epoch, however, I do not mean to detain you; but the room you first entered, into which I will now ask you to return, is full of pictures which you will find interesting if you have time to decipher them, and care for Christianity and its expressions. One only I will ask you to look at, after Titian's Assumption ; the little Ascension by Nicolò Semitecolo, low down, on the right of the vicar's picture in Number 16. For that Ascension is painted in real belief that the Ascension *did* take place; and its sincerity ought to be pleasant to you, after Titian's pretence.

Now, returning up the steps, and taking the corridor to your right, opposite the porter's table, enter the little room through the first door on your right; and therein, just on your left as you go in, is Mantegna's St. George, No. 273. To which, give ten minutes quietly, and examine it with a magnifying glass of considerable power. For in that you have a perfect type of the Italian methods of execution corresponding to the finish of the Dutch painters in the north; but far more intellectual and skilful. You cannot see more wonderful work, in minute drawing with the point of the brush; the virtue of it being that not only every touch is microscopically minute, but that, in this minuteness, every touch is considered, and every touch right. It is to be regarded, however, only as a piece of workmanship. It is wholly without sentiment, though the distant landscape becomes affecting through its detailed truth,—the winding road under the rocks, and the towered city, being as full of little pretty things to be searched out as a natural scene would be.

And I have brought you first, in our now more complete review, to this picture, because it shows more clearly than any other through what tremendous work the Italian masters obtained their power.

Without the inherited strength won by this precision of drawing in the earlier masters, neither Titian nor Tintoret could have existed.

Return into the corridor, and walk along it to the end without wasting time;—there is a Bonifazio, No. 326, worth a painter's while to stop at, but in general mere Dutch rubbish. Walk straight on, and go in at the last door on the left, within which you will find

456, Cima da Conegliano. An entirely sincere and noble picture of the central epoch. Not supreme in any artistic quality, but good and praiseworthy in all; and, as a conception of its subject, the most beautiful you will find in Venice. Grudge no time upon *it;* but look at nothing else here; return into the corridor, and proceed by it into the great room.

Opposite you is Titian's great 'Presentation of the Virgin,' interesting to artists, and an unusually large specimen of Titian's rough work. To me, simply the most stupid and uninteresting picture ever painted by him;—if you can find anything to enjoy in it, you are very welcome: I have nothing more to say of it, except that the colour of the landscape is as false as a piece of common blue tapestry, and that the 'celebrated' old woman with her basket of eggs is as dismally ugly and vulgar a filling of spare corner as was ever daubed on a side-scene in a hurry at Drury Lane.

On the other side of the room, 543, is another wide waste of canvas; miserable example of the work subsequent to Paul Veronese; doubly and trebly mischievous in caricaturing and defiling all that in the master himself is noble: to look long at such a thing is enough to make the truest lovers of Venetian art ashamed of Venice, and of themselves. It ought to be taken down and burned.

Turn your back to it, in the centre of the room; and make up your mind for a long stand; for opposite you, so standing, is a Veronese indeed, of the most instructive and noble kind (489); and beneath it, the best picture in the Academy of Venice, Carpaccio's 'Presentation' (488).

Of the Veronese, I will say nothing but that the main instructiveness of it is in the exhibition of his acquired and inevitable faults (the infection of his æra), with his own quietest and best virtues. It is an artist's picture, and even, only to be rightly felt by very good artists; the aerial perspectives in it being extremely subtle, and rare, to equal degree, in the painter's work. To the general spectator, I will only observe that he has free leave to consider the figure of the Virgin execrable; but that I hope, if he has a good opera-glass, he will find something to please him in the little rose-bush in the glass vase on the balustrade. I would myself give all the bushes—not to say all the trees—and all the seas, of Claude and Poussin, in one bunch and one deluge—for this little rose-bush and its bottle.

488. 'The Presentation in the Temple.' Signed 'Victor Carpaccio, 1510.' From the Church of St. Job.

You have no similar leave, however, good general spectator, to find fault with anything *here!* You may measure yourself, outside and in,—your religion, your taste, your knowledge of art, your knowledge of men and things,—by the quantity of admiration which honestly, after due time given, you can feel for this picture.

You are not required to think the Madonna pretty, or to receive the same religious delight from the conception of the scene, which you would rightly receive from Angelico, Filippo Lippi, or Perugino. This is essentially Venetian,—prosaic, matter of fact, —retaining its supreme common-sense through all enthusiasm.

Nor are you required to think this a first-rate work in Venetian colour. This is the best picture in the Academy precisely because it is *not* the best piece of colour there;—because the great master has subdued his own main passion, and restrained his colour-faculty, though the best in Venice, that you might *not* say the moment you came before the picture, as you do of the Paris Bordone (492), ' *What* a piece of colour ! '

To Paris, the Duke, the Senate, and the Miracle are all merely vehicles for flashes of scarlet and gold on marble and silk; but Carpaccio, in this picture of the Presentation, does not want you to think of *his* colour, but of *your* Christ.

To whom the Madonna also is subjected ;—to whom all is subjected: you will not find such another Infant Christ in Venice ;. (but always look carefully at Paul Veronese's, for it is one of the most singular points in the character of this usually decorative and inexpressive painter, that his Infant Christs are always beautiful).

For the rest, I am not going to praise Carpaccio's work. Give time to it; and if you don't delight in it—the essential faculty of enjoying good art is wanting in you, and I can't give it you by ten minutes' talk; but if you begin really to feel the picture, observe that its supreme merit is in the exactly just balance of all virtue ;—detail perfect, yet inconspicuous; composition intricate and severe, but concealed under apparent simplicity; and painter's faculty of the supremest, used nevertheless with entire subjection of it to intellectual purpose. Titian, compared to Carpaccio, paints as a circus-rider rides,

—there is nothing to be thought of in him but his riding. But Carpaccio paints as a good knight rides; his riding is the least of him; and to himself—unconscious in its ease.

When you have seen all you can of the picture as a whole, go near, and make out the little pictures on the edge of St. Simeon's robe ; four quite lovely ones ; the lowest admitting, to make the whole perfect, delightful grotesque of fairy angels within a heavenly castle wall, thrusting down a troop of supine devils to the deep. The other three, more beautiful in their mystery of shade; but I have not made them out yet. There is one solemn piece of charge to a spirit folding its arms in obedience ; and I think the others must be myths of creation, but can't tell yet, and must now go on quickly to note merely the pictures you should look at, reserving talk of them for a second number of this Guide.

483, 500, 524, containing all you need study in Bonifazio. In 500, he is natural, and does his best ; in 483, he pretends to religion, which he has not ; in 524, to art, which he has not. The last is a monstrous example of the apathy with which the later Italian artists, led by Raphael, used this horrible subject to exhibit their ingenuity in anatomical posture, and excite the feeble interest of vulgar spectators.

503. Quiet Tintoret; very noble in senators, poor in Madonna.

519. Quiet Paul Veronese; very noble in St. Jerome's robe and Lion, and in little St. John's back. Not particularly so in anybody's front, but a first-rate picture in the picture-way.

507. Dashing Tintoret: fearfully repainted, but grand yet in the lighter figures of background.

496—502. Dashing Paul Veronese — splendid in art; in conception of Evangelists—all that Venice wanted of them, at that day. You must always, however, judge her as you would a sailor,—what would be ridiculous or bombastic in others has often some honesty in it with *her*. Think of these Evangelists as a kind of figure-heads of ships.

Enter now the great room with the Veronese at the end of it, for which the painter (quite rightly) was summoned before the Inquisition of State : you will find his examination, translated by a friend to whom I owe much in my old Venetian days, in the Appendix to my second Guide; but you must not stop now at this picture, if you are in a hurry, for you can see the like of it, and better, in Paris; but you can see nothing in all the world, out of Venice, like certain other pictures in this room.

Glancing round it, you see it may be generally described as full of pictures of street architecture, with various more or less interesting transactions going on in the streets. Large Canalettos, in fact; only with the figures a little more interesting than Canaletto's figures; and the buildings, on the whole, red and white or brown and white, instead of, as with Canaletto, black and white. And on consideration, and observation, you will perceive, if you *have* any perception of colour, that Venetian buildings, and most others, being really red and white or brown and white, not black and white, this is really the right manner of painting them, and these are true and sufficient representations of streets, of landscapes, and of interiors of houses, with the people, as I said, either in St. Mark's Place, 555, or at Grand Cairo, 540, or before the Castle of St. Angelo at Rome, 546, or by the old Rialto here, 564, being themselves also more or less interesting, if you will observe them, first in their dresses, which are very curious and pretty, and afterwards in many other particulars, of which for the present I must leave you to make out what you can; for of the pictures by Carpaccio in this room I must write an entirely separate account, (begun already for one of them only, the Dream of St. Orsola, 533,)* and of the Gentile

* Of which, with her legend, if you care to hear more, you will find more in the three numbers of 'Fors Clavigera' now purchaseable of my agent in Venice.

Bellini you can only know the value after good study of St. Mark's itself. Observe, however, at least in this, and in 548 and 564, the perfectly true representation of what the Architecture of Venice was in her glorious time; trim, dainty,— red and white like the blossom of a carnation, —touched with gold like a peacock's plumes, and frescoed, even to its chimney-pots, with fairest arabesque,—its inhabitants, and it together, one harmony of work and life,—all of a piece, you see them, in the wonderful palace-perspective on the left in 548, with everybody looking out of their windows. And in this picture of St. Mark's, painted by John Bellini's good brother, true as he could, hue for hue, and ray for ray, you see that all the tossing of its *now* white marble foliage against the sky, which in my old book on Venice I compared to the tossed spray of sea waves, (believing then, as I do still, that the Venetians in their living and breathing days of art were always influenced in their choice of guiding lines of sculpture by their sense of the action of wind or sea,) were not, at all events, meant to be like sea foam white in anger, but like light spray in morning sunshine. They were all overlaid with gold.

Not yet in vicious luxury. Those porches of St. Mark's, so please you, English friends, were not thus gilt for the wedding of Miss Kilmansegg, nor

are those pictures on the vaults, advertisements,
like yours in your railway stations;—all the arts
of England bent on recommending you cheap
bathing machines and painless pills. Here are purer
baths and medicines told of; here have been more
ingenious engineers. From the Sinai desert, from
the Sion rock, from the defiles of Lebanon, met
here the ghosts of ancient builders to oversee the
work,—of dead nations, to inspire it: Bezaleel and
the maids of Israel who gave him their jewels;
Hiram and his forgers in the vale of Siddim—his
woodmen of the Syrian forests;—David the lord of
war, and his son the Lord of Peace, and the mul-
titudes that kept holyday when the cloud filled
the house they had built for the Lord of All;—
these, in their myriads stood by, to watch, to
guide;—it might have been, had Venice willed, to
bless.

Literally so, mind you. The wreathen work of
the lily capitals and their archivolts, the glass that
keeps unfaded their colour—the design of that
colour itself, and the stories that are told in the
glow of it,—all these were brought by the Jew or
the Tyrian, bringing also the treasures of Persia
and Egypt; and with these, labouring beside them
as one brought up with them, stood the Athena
of Corinth, and the Sophia of Byzantium.

Not in vicious luxury these, yet—though in

Tyrian splendour glows St. Mark's;—nor those
quiet and trim little houses on the right, joining
the Campanile. You are standing, (the work is so
completely done that you may soon fancy yourself
so,) in old St. Mark's Place, at the far end of it,
before it was enlarged; you may find the stone
marking the whole length of it in the pavement,
just opposite the easternmost door of the Café
Florian. And there were none of those pompous
loggie then, where you walk up and down before
the café, but these trim, dainty, happily-inhabited
houses, mostly in white marble and gold, with
disks of porphyry;—and look at the procession
coming towards you underneath them—what a bed
of moving flowers it is! Not Birnam wood coming,
gloomy and terrible, but a very bloom and garland
of good and knightly manhood—its Doge walking
in the midst of it—simple, valiant, actual, bene-
ficent, magnificent king. Do you see better sights
than this in St. Mark's Place now, in your days
of progress?

Now, just to get some little notion how the
figures are 'put in' by these scrupulous old for-
malists, take the pains to look closely at the first
you come upon, of the procession on the extreme
left,—the three musicians, namely, with the harp,
violin, and lute. Look at them as portraits only:
you will not find more interesting ones in all the

rooms.　And then you will do well to consider
the picture as a reality for a little while, and so
leave the Academy with a vision of living Venice
in your heart.　We will look at no more painting,
to-day.

GUIDE, ETC.

PART II.

IF you have looked with care at the three musicians, or any other of the principal figures, in the great town or landscape views in this principal room, you will be ready now with better patience to trace the order of their subjects, and such character or story as their treatment may develope. I can only help you, however, with Carpaccio's, for I have not been able to examine, or much think of, Mansueti's, recognizing nevertheless much that is delightful in them.

By Carpaccio, then, in this room,* there are in all eleven important pictures, eight from the legend of St. Ursula, and three of distinct subjects. Glance first at the series of St. Ursula subjects, in this order :—

I.—539. Maurus the king of Britany receives

* Or at least in the Academy : the arrangement may perhaps be altered before this Guide can be published ; at all events we must not count on it.

the English ambassadors ; and has talk with his daughter touching their embassy.

II.—533. St. Ursula's Dream.

III.—537. King Maurus dismisses the English ambassadors with favourable answer from his daughter. (This is the most beautiful piece of *painting* in the rooms.)

IV.—549. The King of England receives the Princess's favourable answer.

V.—542. The Prince of England sets sail for Britany ;—there receives his bride, and embarks with her on pilgrimage.

VI.—546. The Prince of England and his bride, voyaging on pilgrimage with the eleven thousand maidens, arrive at Rome, and are received by the Pope, who, " with certain Cardinals," joins their pilgrimage. (The most beautiful of all the series, next to the Dream.)

VII.—554. The Prince, with his bride, and the Pope with his Cardinals, and the eleven thousand maids, arrive in the land of the Huns, and receive martyrdom there. In the second part of the picture is the funeral procession of St. Ursula.

VIII.—St. Ursula, with her maidens, and the pilgrim Pope, and certain Cardinals, in glory of Paradise. I have always forgotten to look for the poor bridegroom in this picture, and on looking, am by no means sure of him. But I suppose it is he who holds St. Ursula's standard. The architecture and landscape are unsurpassably fine; the rest much imperfect; but containing nobleness only to be learned by long dwelling on it.

In this series, I have omitted one picture, 544, which is of scarcely any interest—except in its curious faults and unworthiness. At all events, do not at present look at it, or think of it; but let us examine all the rest without hurry.

In the first place, then, we find this curious fact, intensely characteristic of the fifteenth as opposed to the nineteenth century—that the figures are true and natural, but the landscape false and unnatural, being by such fallacy made entirely subordinate to the figures. I have never approved' of, and only a little understand, this state of things. The painter is never interested in the ground, but only in the creatures that tread on it. A castle tower is left a mere brown bit of canvas, and all his colouring kept for the trumpeters on the top of it. The fields are obscurely green; the sky imperfectly blue; and the mountains could not possibly stand on the very small foundations they are furnished with.

Here is a Religion of Humanity, and nothing else,—to purpose! Nothing in the universe thought worth a look, unless it is in service or foil to some

two-legged creature showing itself off to the best
advantage. If a flower is in a girl's hair, it shall
be painted properly; but in the fields, shall be only
a spot : if a striped pattern is on a boy's jacket,
we paint all the ins and outs of it, and drop not
a stitch; but the striped patterns of vineyard or
furrow in field, the enamelled mossy mantles of the
rocks, the barred heraldry of the shield of the sky,
—perhaps insects and birds may take pleasure in
them, not we. To his own native lagunes and sea,
the painter is yet less sensitive. His absurd rocks,
and dotty black hedges round bitumen-coloured
fields, (542,) are yet painted with some grotesque
humour, some modest and unworldly beauty; and
sustain or engird their castellated quaintnesses in a
manner pleasing to the pre-Raphaelite mind. But
the sea—waveless as a deal board—and in that
tranquillity, for the most part reflecting nothing at
its edge,—literally, such a sea justifies that un-
courteous saying of earlier Venice of her Doge's
bride,—" Mare sub pede pono."*

Of all these deficiencies, characteristic not of
this master only, but of his age, you will find

---

* On the scroll in the hand of the throned Venice on the Piazzetta
ide of the Ducal Palace, the entire inscription is,

" Fortis, justa, trono furias, mare sub pede, pono."

" Strong, and just, I put the furies beneath my throne, and the sea
beneath my foot."

various analysis in the third volume of 'Modern Painters,' in the chapter on mediæval landscape; with begun examination of the causes which led gradually to more accurate observance of natural phenomena, until, by Turner, the method of Carpaccio's mind is precisely reversed, and the Nature in the background becomes principal; the figures in the foreground, its foil. I have a good deal more, however, to say on this subject now,—so much more, indeed, that in this little Guide there is no proper room for any of it, except the simple conclusion that both the painters are wrong in whatever they either definitely misrepresent, or enfeeble by inharmonious deficiency.

In the next place, I want you to notice Carpaccio's fancy in what he does represent very beautifully,—the architecture, real and ideal, of his day.

His fancy, I say; or phantasy; the notion he has of what architecture should be; of which, without doubt, you see his clearest expression in the Paradise, and in the palace of the most Christian King, St. Ursula's father.

And here I must ask you to remember, or learn if you do not know, the general course of transition in the architecture of Venice;—namely, that there are three epochs of good building in Venice; the first lasting to 1300, Byzantine, in the style of

St. Mark's; the second, 1300 to 1480, Gothic, in the style of the Ducal Palace; and the third, 1480 to 1520, in a manner which architects have yet given no entirely accepted name to, but which, from the name of its greatest designer, Brother Giocondo, of Verona,* I mean, myself, henceforward to call ' Giocondine.'

Now the dates on these pictures of Carpaccio's run from 1480 to 1485, so that you see he was painting in the youthful gush, as it were, and fullest impetus of Giocondine architecture, which all Venice, and chiefly Carpaccio, in the joy of art, thought was really at last the architecture divinely designed, and arrived at by steady progress of taste, from the Creation to 1480, and then the ne plus ultra, and real Babel-style without bewilderment —its top truly reaching to heaven,—style which was never thenceforth to be bettered by human thought or skill. Of which Giocondine manner, I really think you had better at once see a substantially existent piece. It will not take long,—say an hour, with lunch; and the good door-keeper will let you come in again without paying.†

So, (always supposing the day fine,) go down to

* Called " the second Founder of Venice," for his engineering work on the Brenta. His architecture is chiefly at Verona; the style being adopted and enriched at Venice by the Lombardi.

† If you have already seen the school of St. John, or do not like the interruption, continue at page 89.

your boat, and order yourself to be taken to the church of the Frari. Landing just beyond it, your gondoliers will show you the way, up the calle beside it, to the desolate little courtyard of the School of St. John the Evangelist. It might be one of the most beautiful scenes among the cities of Italy, if only the good Catholics of Venice would employ so much of their yearly alms in the honour of St. John the Evangelist as to maintain any old gondolier, past rowing, in this courtyard by way of a Patmos, on condition that he should suffer no wildly neglected children to throw stones at the sculptures, nor grown-up creatures to defile them; but with occasional ablution by sprinkling from garden-water engine, suffer the weeds of Venice to inhabit among the marbles where they listed.

How beautiful the place might be, I need not tell you. Beautiful it is, even in its squalid misery; but too probably, some modern designer of railroad stations will do it up with new gilding and scrapings of its grey stone. The gods forbid ;—understand, at all events, that if this happens to it, you are no more to think of it as an example of Giocondine art. But, as long as it is let alone there, in the shafts and capitals you will see on the whole the most characteristic example in Venice of the architecture that Carpaccio, Cima, and John Bellini loved.

As a rule, observe, square-piered, not round-

pillared;—the square piers either sculptured all up
with floral tracery, or, if plain, decorated, half-way
up, by a round panel of dark-coloured marble or
else a bas-relief, usually a classic profile; the
capitals, of light leafage, playing or springing into
joyful spirals at the angles; the mouldings and
cornices on the whole very flat or square cut,—no
solid round mouldings anywhere, but all precise,
rectangular, and shallow. The windows and doors
either square-headed or round,—never pointed; but,
if square-headed, having often a Greek gable or
pediment above, as here on the outer wall; and, if
round-headed, often composed of two semicircles
side by side, with a circle between:* the wall
decoration being either of round inlaid marbles,
among floral sculpture, or of fresco. Little to be
conceived from words; but if you will look well
inside and outside of the cortile of the Evangelist,
you will come away with a very definite primary
notion of Giocondine work.

Then back, with straight speed to the Academy;
and before landing there, since you can see the
little square in front of it, from your boat, read on.

* In returning to your boat, just walk round to the back of the
church of the Frari, and look at the windows of the Scuola di San
Rocco, which will fix the form in your mind. It is an entirely bad
one; but took the fancy of men, for a time, and of strong ones, too.
But don't stop long just now to look at this later building; keep the
St. John's cortile for your type of Giocondine work, pure.

The little square has its name written up at the corner, you see,—"Field of Charity," or rather of *the* Charity, meaning the Madonna of Charity, and church dedicated to her. Of which you see the mere walls, variously defaced, remaining yet in their original form,—traces of the great circular window in the front yet left, also of the pointed windows at the sides—filled up, many a year ago, and the square holes below cut for modern convenience: there being no space in the length and breadth of Italy to build new square-holed houses on, the Church of Charity must be used for makeshift.

Have you charity of imagination enough to cover this little field with fresh grass,—to tear down the iron bridge which some accursed Englishman, I suppose, greedy for filthy job, persuaded the poor Venetians to spoil their Grand Canal with, at its noblest bend,—and to fill the pointed lateral windows with light tracery of quatrefoiled stone? So stood, so bloomed, the church and its field, in early fourteenth century—dismal time! the church in its fresh beauty then, built towards the close of the thirteenth century, on the site of a much more ancient one, first built of wood; and, in 1119, ot stone; but still very small, its attached monastery receiving Alexander III. in 1177;—here on the little flowery field landed the Pontiff Exile, whose foot was to tread so soon on the Lion and the Adder.

And, some hundred years later, putting away, one finds not why, her little Byzantine church, more gravely meditative Venice, visited much by Dominican and Franciscan friars, and more or less in cowled temper herself, built this graver and simpler pile; which, if any of my readers care for either Turner or me, they should look at with some moments' pause; for I have given Turner's lovely sketch of it to Oxford, painted as he saw it fifty years ago, with bright golden sails grouped in front of it where now is the ghastly iron bridge.*

Most probably, (I cannot yet find any direct document of it,) the real occasion of the building of the church whose walls yet stand, was the founding of the Confraternita di S. Maria della Carità, on St. Leonard's Day, 6th November, 1260,† which brotherhood, in 1310, fought side by side with the school of the Painters in St. Luke's field, against one body of the conspirators for Bajamonte, and drove them back, achieving the right thenceforward of planting their purple standard there, in

* 'Very convenient for the people,' say you, modern man of business. Yes; very convenient to them also to pay two centesimi every time they cross,—six for three persons, into the pockets of that English engineer; instead of five for three persons, to one of their own boatmen, who now take to begging, drinking, and bellowing for the wretched hordes at the table d'hôtes, whose ears have been rent by railroad whistles till they don't know a howl from a song,—instead of ferrying.

† Archivio Veneto. (Venezia, 1876.) Tom. XII., Parte i., p. 112.

St. Luke's field, with their stemma; (all this bears on Carpaccio's pictures presently, so have patience yet a minute or two), and so increasing in number and influence, bought in 1344, from the Monks of the Church of Charity, the ground on which you are presently going to see pictures; and built on it their cloister, dedicated also to St. Mary of Charity; and over the gate of it, by which you are going to enter, put St. Mary of Charity, as they best could get her carved, next year, 1345: and so you have her there, with cowled members of the confraternity kneeling to her; happy angels fluttering about her; the dark blue of her eyes not yet utterly faded from them. Blue-eyed as Athena she,—the Greek tradition yet prevailing to that extent,—a perfect type, the whole piece, of purest central fourteenth-century Gothic thought and work, untouched, and indubitable of date, being inscribed below its bracket cornice,

MCCCXLV. Ī LO TEMPO DE MIS.

MARCHO ZULIAN FO FATO STO LAVORIER.

To wit—"1345, in the time" (of the Guardian-ship) "of Messer Mark Julian, was made this laboured thing."

And all seemed to bid fair for Venice and her sacred schools; Heaven surely pleased with these her endeavours, and laboured things.

Yes, with these, and such other, I doubt not. But other things, it seems, had been done in Venice, with which Heaven was *not* pleased; assuming always that there is a Heaven, for otherwise—what followed was of course only process of Darwinian development. But this *was* what followed. That Madonna, with her happy angels and humble worshippers, was carved as you see her, over the Scuola cloister door,—in 1345. And "on the 25th of January, 1347,* on the day, to wit, of the conversion of St. Paul, about the hour of vespers, there came a great earthquake in Venice, and as it were in all the world; and fell many tops of bell-towers, and houses, and chimneys, and the church of St. Basil: and there was so great fear that all the people thought to die. And the earth ceased not to tremble for about forty days; and when it remained quiet, there came a great mortality, and the people died of various evil. And the people were in so great fear, that father would not go to visit son, nor son father. And this death lasted about six months; and it was said commonly that there died two parts out of three, of all the people of Venice."

These words you may read, (in Venetian dialect,) after you have entered the gate beneath the Madonna; they are engraved under the Gothic

---

* 1848, in our present calendar.

arch on your right hand; with other like words, telling the various horror of that Plague; and how the guardian of the Scuola died by it, and about ten of his officers with him, and three hundred of the brethren.

Above the inscription, two angels hold the symbol of the Scuola; carved, as you see, conspicuously also on the outer sculptures in various places; and again on the well in the midst of the cloister. The first sign this, therefore, of all chosen by the greater schools of Venice, of which, as aforesaid, "The first was that of St. Mary of Charity, which school has its wax candles red, in sign that Charity should be glowing; and has for its bearing a yellow" (meaning golden*) " cross, traversing two little circles also yellow; with red and green quartering the parts which the cross describes,—those who instituted such sign desiring to show thereby the union that Charity should have with Faith and Hope." †

The golden ' anchored ' cross stands for Faith, the golden outer circle for Charity, the golden inner for Hope—all on field quartered gules and vert, the colours of Charity and Hope.

---

* Ex Cruce constat aurea, seu flava; ejus speciei, quam artis hujusmodi Auctores ' ancoratam ' vocant.

† In tabulam Græcam insigni sodalitio S. M. Caritatis, Venetiarum, ab amplissimo Cardinali Bessarione dono datam, Dissertatio.—(St. Mark's library, 33931, page 146.)

Such the first symbol of Venetian Brother-hoods,*—in reading which, I delay you, that you may be better prepared to understand the symbolism running through every sign and colour in Venetian art at this time, down even to its tinting of wax candles; art which was indeed all the more symbolic for being rude, and complicated much with the use of signals and heraldries at sea, too distant for any art in them to be visible, but serviceably intelligible in meaning.

How far the great Scuola and cloisters of the Carita, for monks and confraternity together, reached from the gate under which you are pausing, you may see in Durer's woodcut of the year 1500, (Correr Museum,) which gives the apse with attached chapels; and the grand double cloister reaching back nearly to the Giudecca; a water-wheel—as I suppose—outside, on the (now filled up and paved) canal, moved by the tide, for molinary work in the kitchens. Of all which nothing now remains but these pillars and beams, between you and the gallery staircase; and the well, with two brothers on each side holding their Stemma, a fine free-hand piece of rough living work. You will not, I think, find that you have ill spent your

---

* At least according to the authority above quoted; as far as I have consulted the original documents myself, I find the school of St. Theodore primal.

hour of rest when you now return into the Carpaccio room, where we will look first, please, at
No. IV. (549), in which many general points are
better shown than in the rest.

Here is the great King of ideal England, under
an octagonal temple of audience; all the scene
being meant to show the conditions of a state in
perfect power and prosperity.

A state, therefore, that is at once old and young;
that has had a history for centuries past, and will
have one for centuries to come.

Ideal, founded mainly on the Venice of his own
day; mingled a little with thoughts of great Rome,
and of great antagonist Genoa: but, in all spirit
and hope, the Venice of 1480—1500 is here living
before you. And now, therefore, you can see at
once what she meant by a 'Campo,' allowing
for the conventional manner of representing grass,
which of course at first you will laugh at; but
which is by no means deserving of your con-
tempt. Any hack draughtsman of Dalziel's can
sketch for you, or any member of the Water-colour
or Dudley Societies dab for you, in ten minutes, a
field of hay that you would fancy you could mow,
and make cocks of. But this green ground of
Carpaccio's, with implanted flowers and tufts of
grass, is traditional from the first Greek-Christian
mosaics, and is an entirely systematic ornamental

2

ground, and to be understood as such, primarily,
and as grass only symbolically. Careless indeed,
more than is usual with him—much spoiled and
repainted also; but quite clear enough in expression for us of the orderliness and freshness
of a Venetian campo in the great times; garden
and city you see mingled inseparably, the wild
strawberry growing at the steps of the king's
court of justice, and their marble sharp and
bright out of the turf. Clean everything, and
pure;—no cigars in anybody's poisoned mouth,—
no voiding of perpetual excrement of saliva on the
precious marble or living flowers. Perfect peace
and befittingness of behaviour in all men and
creatures. Your very monkey in repose, perfect
in his mediæval dress; the Darwinian theory in
all its sacredness, breadth, divinity, and sagacity,
—but reposeful, not venturing to thrust itself into
political council. Crowds on the bridges and quays,
but untumultuous, close set as beds of flowers,
richly decorative in their mass, and a beautiful
mosaic of men, and of black, red, blue, and golden
bonnets. Ruins, indeed, among the prosperity; but
glorious ones;—not shells of abandoned ‍speculation, but remnants of mighty state long ago, now
restored to nature's peace; the arches of the first
bridge the city had built, broken down by storm,
yet what was left of them spared for memory's

sake. (So stood for a little while, a few years ago, the broken Ponte-a-Mare at Pisa; so at Rome, for ages, stood the Ponte Rotto, till the engineers and modern mob got at it, making what was in my youth the most lovely and holy scene in Rome, *now* a place where a swineherd could not stand without holding his nose, and which no woman can stop at.)

But here, the old arches are covered with sweet weeds, like native rock, and (for once!) reflected a little in the pure water under the meadowy hills. Much besides of noteworthy, if you are yourself worthy of noting it, you may find in this lovely distance. But the picture, it may be complained, seems for the most part—distance, architecture, and scattered crowd; while of foreground objects, we have principally cloaks, and very curiously thin legs.* Well, yes,—the distance is indeed the prettiest part of this picture; and since, in modern art and drama, we have been accustomed, for anatomical and other reasons, to depend on nothing else but legs, I admit the supply of legs to be here scanty, and even of brachial, pectoral, and other admirable muscles. If you choose to look at the *faces* instead, you will find something in them; nevertheless, Carpaccio has been, on the

* Not in the least unnaturally thin, however, in the forms of persons of sedentary life.

whole, playing with himself, and with us, in his treatment of this subject. For Carpaccio is, in the most vital and conclusive sense, a man of genius, who will not at all supply you, nor can in the least supply himself, with sublimity and pathos to order; but is sublime, or delightful, or sometimes dull, or frequently grotesque, as Heaven wills it; or—profane persons will say,—as the humour takes him. And his humour here has been dominant. For since much depends on the answer brought back from St. Ursula, besides the young Prince's happiness, one should have thought, the return of the embassy might have been represented in a loftier manner. But only two of the ambassadors are here; the king is occupied in hearing a cause which will take long,—(see how gravely his minister is reading over the documents in question;)—meantime the young prince, impatient, going down the steps of the throne, makes his own private inquiries, proudly: "Your embassy has, I trust, been received, gentlemen, with a just understanding of our diplomatic relations?" "Your Royal Highness," the lowly and gravely bowing principal ambassador replies, "must yourself be the only fitting judge of that matter, on fully hearing our report." Meantime, the chargé d'affaires holds St. Ursula's answer—behind his back.

A piece of play, very nearly, the whole picture;

a painter living in the midst of a prosperous city, happy in his own power, entirely believing in God, and in the saints, and in eternal life; and, at intervals, bending his whole soul to the expression of most deep and holy tragedy,—such a man needs must have his times of play; which Carpaccio takes, in his work. Another man, instead of painting this piece with its monkey, and its little fiddler, and its jesting courtiers, would have played some ape-tricks of his own,—spent an hour or two among literal fiddlers, and living courtiers. Carpaccio is not heard of among such—amuses himself still with pencil in hand, and us also, pleasantly, for a little while. You shall be serious enough, soon, with him, if you will.

But I find this Guide must run into greater division, for I can't get the end of it properly done yet for some days; during the winter the gallery was too cold for me to think quietly in, and so I am obliged, as Fate always lately obliges me, to do this work from pen to print—at speed; so that, quitting Carpaccio for the nonce, I will tell you a little more about the general contents of the rooms; and so afterwards take up St. Ursula's pilgrimage, undisturbed.* Now, therefore, I will

* This I am now doing in a separate Guide to the works of Carpaccio in Venice: these two parts, now published, contain all I have to say about the Academy.

simply follow the order of the room circuit, noting the pieces worth study, if you have proper time.

From before this picture which has so long held us, go down the steps on the right of it, into the lower room.

Turning round immediately, you have good sight of two Paul Veroneses, one on each side of the steps. The upper group of the picture on your left, (603), Madonna borne by angels at her knees, and encompassed by a circlet of them, is the loveliest piece of Veronese in these galleries, nor can you see a better in the world: but, considered as a whole, the picture is a failure; all the sub-celestial part of it being wholly dull. Nevertheless, for essential study of Veronese's faculty, you cannot find anything better in Venice than that upper group; and the opposite picture, though confused, is worth attentive pause from all painters.

597. Le Brun. Sent from Paris, you see, in exchange for the Cena of Paul Veronese.

The Cena of Paul Veronese being worth—at moderate estimate of its eternal and intrinsic art-value—I should say, roughly, about ten good millions of sterling ducats, or twenty ironclads; and the Le Brun, worth, if it were put to proper use, precisely what its canvas may now be worth to make a packing-case of;—but, as hung here, in

negative value, and effectual mischief, in disgracing
the rooms, and keeping fine pictures invisibly out
of the way,—a piece of vital poverty and calamity
much more than equivalent to the presence of a
dirty, torn rag, which the public would at once
know to be worthless, in its place instead.

569, 570. Standard average portrait-pieces, fairly
representative of Tintoret's quiet work, and of
Venetian magistrates,—Camerlenghi di Comune.
Compare 587; very beautiful.

581, 582, 583. Spoils of the Church of the
Carita, whose ruins you have seen. Venice being
of all cities the only one which has sacked *herself*,
not in revolution, but mere blundering beggary;
suppressing every church that had blessed her,
and every society that had comforted. But at all
events you *see* the pictures here: and the Cima
is a fine one; but what time you give to this
painter should be spent chiefly with his John the
Baptist at the Madonna dell' Orto.

586. Once a Bonifazio of very high order; sorrow-
fully repainted with loss of half its life. But a
picture, still, deserving honour.

From this room you find access either to the
modern pictures, or by the door on the left hand

of the Cima, to the collection of drawings. The well-known series by Raphael and Lionardo are of the very highest historical value and artistic interest; but it is curious to find, in Venice, scarcely a scratch or blot remaining of elementary study by any great Venetian master. Her painters drew little in black and white, and must have thrown such sketches, when they made them, away for mere waste paper. For all discussion of their methods of learning to draw with colour from the first, I must refer my readers to my Art lectures.

The Lionardo drawings here are the finest I know; none in the Ambrosian library equal them in execution.

The staircase leading out of this room descends into the Hall of Titian's Assumption, where I have said nothing yet of his last picture (33), nor of that called in the Guide-books an example of his first style (35).

It has always been with me an intended piece of work to trace the real method of Titian's study, and the changes of his mind. But I shall never do it now;* and am hitherto entirely unacquainted with his early work. If this be indeed his, and a juvenile piece, it indicates a breadth of manner, and conventionally artistic way of looking at nature,

* For reasons which any acute reader may enough discover in my lecture on Michael Angelo and Tintoret.

entirely peculiar to him, or to his æra. The picture which he left unfinished might most fittingly be called the Shadow of Death. It is full of the profoundest metaphysical interest to me; but cannot be analysed here.

In general, Titian is ill-represented in his own Venice. The best example of him, by far, is the portrait group of the Pesaro family in the Frari. The St. Mark in the Sacristy of the Salute was, in my early days, entirely glorious; but has been daubed over into ruin. The roof of the Sacristy in the Salute; with the fresco of St. Christopher,* and the portrait of the Doge Grimani before Faith, in the Ducal Palace, are all the remnants of him that are worth study here, since the destruction of the Peter Martyr.† The St. John the Baptist in this gallery (366), is really too stupid to be endured, and the black and white scrabble of landscape in it is like a bad copy of Ruysdael.

45. The miracle of St. Mark; a fine, but muchoverrated, Tintoret. If any painter of real power

---

* An admirable account of this fresco is given by Mr. Edward Cheney, in ' Original Documents relating to Venetian Painters and their Pictures in the Eighteenth Century,' pp. 60, 61.

† Of the portrait of the Doge Andrea Gritti, in my own possession at Oxford, I leave others to speak, when I can speak of it no more. But it must be named here as the only fragment left of another great picture destroyed by fire, which Tintoret had so loved and studied that he replaced it from memory.

wishes to study this master, let him be content with the Paradise of the Ducal Palace, and the School of St. Roch, where no harmful repainting has yet taken place. The once mighty pictures in the Madonna dell' Orto are destroyed by restoration; and those which are scattered about the other churches are scarcely worth pursuit, while the series of St. Roch remains in its purity.

In the next room to this, (Sala III.,) the pictures on the ceiling, brought from the room of the State Inquisitors, are more essential, because more easy, Tintoret-work, than the St. Mark, and very delightful to me; I only wish the Inquisitors were alive to enjoy them again themselves, and inquire into a few things happening in Venice, and especially into the religious principles of her "Modern Painters."

We have made the round of the rooms, all but the Pinacoteca Contarini, Sala V. and VI., and the long gallery, Sala X.—XIV., both containing many smaller pictures of interest; but of which I have no time, nor much care, to speak—except in complaint that detestable daubs by Callot, Dujardin, and various ignoti, should be allowed to disgrace the sixth sala, and occupy some of the best of the very little good light there is in the Academy; thrusting the lovely little Tintoret, 179,—purest work of his heart and fairest of his faculty,—high beyond sight of all its delicious painting; and the excellent quiet portrait, 168, into an unregarded corner. I am always puzzled by the smaller pictures of John Bellini; many of them here, of whose authorship there can be little doubt, being yet of very feeble merit. 94 is fine; the five symbolical pictures, 234—238, in the inner room, Sala VI., are interesting to myself; but may probably be little so to others. The first is, (I believe,) Domestic Love; the world in her hand becoming the colour of Heaven; the second, Fortitude quitting the effeminate Dionysus; the third, (much the poorest and least intelligible,) Truth, or Prudence; the fourth, Lust; and the fifth, Fortune as Opportunity, in distinction from the greater and sacred Fortune appointed of Heaven.

And now, if you are yet unfatigued,* you had better go back into the great room, and give thorough examination to the wonderful painting, as such, in the great Veronese, considering what all its shows and dexterities at last came to, and reading, before it, his examination concerning it, given in Appendix, which shows you that Venice herself felt what they were likely to come to, though in vain; and then, for contrast with its reckless power, and for final image to be remembered of sweet Italian art in its earnestness, return into the long gallery, (through the two great rooms, turning

* If you *are*, end with 179, and remember it well.

your back on the Veronese, then out by the door opposite Titian's huge picture; then out of the corridor by the first door on the right, and walk down the gallery,) to its little Sala X., where, high on your left, 360, is the Beata Catherine Vigri's St. Ursula; Catherine Vigri herself, it may be, kneeling to her. Truly a very much blessed Catherine, and, I should say, far more than half-way to a saint, knowing, however, of her, and her work, only this picture. Of which I will only say in closing, as I said of the Vicar's picture in beginning, that it would be well if any of us could do such things nowadays;—and more especially, if our vicars and young ladies could.

APPENDIX.

THE little collection of 'documents relating to Venetian painters' already referred to (p. 47), as made with excellent judgment by Mr. Edward Cheney, is, I regret to say, 'communicated' only to the author's friends, of whom I, being now one of long standing, emboldened also by repeated instances of help received from him, venture to trespass on the modest book so far as to reprint part of the translation which it gives of the questioning of Paul Veronese.

"It is well known," says Mr. Cheney in his prefatory remarks, "to the students of Venetian history, that the Roman Inquisition was allowed little influence, and still less power, in the states of the Signory; and its sittings were always attended by lay members, selected from the Senate, to regulate and report its proceedings.

"The sittings of the Holy Office were held in the chapel of St. Theodore, fronting the door leading from St. Mark's Church to the Fondamenta di Canonica."

On Saturday, the 8th July, 1573, Master Paul Caliari, of Verona, a painter, residing in the parish of St. Samuel, was brought before the Sacred Tribunal; and being asked his name and surname, answered as above; and being asked of his profession, answered—

"*A.* I invent and draw figures.

Q. Do you know the reason why you have been summoned?

A. No, my lord.

Q. Can you imagine it?

A. I can imagine it.

Q. Tell us what you imagine.

A. For the reason which the Reverend Prior of SS. Giovanni and Paolo, whose name I know not, told me that he had been here, and that your illustrious lordships had given him orders that I should substitute the figure of the Magdalen for that of a dog; and I replied that I would willingly have done this, or anything else for my own credit and the advantage of the picture, but that I did not think the figure of the Magdalen would be fitting (! !) * or would look well, for many reasons, which I will always assign whenever the opportunity is given me.

Q. What picture is that which you have named?

A. It is the picture representing the last † supper that Jesus took with his disciples in the house of Simon.

Q. Where is this picture?

A. In the refectory of the Friars of SS. Giovanni and Paolo.

* I must interpolate two notes of admiration. After all one has heard of the terrors of the Inquisition, it seems, nevertheless, some people ventured to differ with it in opinion, on occasion. And the Inquisition was entirely right, too. See next note.

† "Cena *ultima* che," etc.: the last, that is to say, of the two which Veronese supposed Christ to have taken with this host; but he had not carefully enough examined the apparently parallel passages. They are confusing enough, and perhaps the reader will be glad to refer to them in their proper order.

I. There is, first, the feast given to Christ by St. Matthew, after he was called; the circumstances of it told by himself; only saying '*the* house' instead of '*my* house' (Matt. ix. 9—13). This is the

Q. Is it painted on the wall, on panel, or on cloth ?

A. On cloth.

Q. How many feet is it in height ?

A. It is about seventeen feet.

Q. How wide ?

A. About thirty-nine feet.

Q. In this Supper of our Lord have you painted any attendants ?

A. Yes, my lord.

feast at which the objection is taken by the Pharisees—" Why eateth your Master with publicans and sinners ? " the event being again related by St. Luke (v. 29), giving Matthew the name of Levi. No other circumstance of interest takes place on this occasion.

II. " One of the Pharisees desired Him that He would eat with him : and He went into the Pharisee's house, and sat down to meat " (Luke viii. 36).

To *this* feast came the Magdalen, and " stood at His feet, behind Him, weeping." And you know the rest. The same lesson given to the Pharisees who *forbade* the feast of Matthew, here given—in how much more pathetic force—to the Pharisee at whose feast Jesus now sat. Another manner of sinner this, who stands uncalled, at the feast, weeping ; who in a little while will stand weeping—not for herself. The name of the Pharisee host is given in Christ's grave address to him—" Simon, I have somewhat to say unto thee."

III. The *supper* at Bethany, in the house of Simon " the Leper," where Lazarus sat at table, where Martha served, and where her sister Mary poured the ointment on Christ's head, " for my burial," (Mark xiv. 3 ; Matt. xxvi. 7 ; and John xii. 2, where in the following third verse doubtless some copyist, confusing her with the Magdalen, added the clause of her wiping His feet with her hair ;—so also, more palpably, in John xi. 2). Here the objection is made by Judas, and the lesson given—" The poor ye have always with you."

We cannot seriously suppose Simon the leper to be the same person as Simon the Pharisee ; still less Simon the Pharisee to be the same as Matthew the publican ; but in Veronese's mind their three feasts had got confused, and he thinks of them as *two* only,

Q. Say how many attendants, and what each is doing.

A. First, the master of the house, Simon; besides, I have placed below him a server, who I have supposed to have come for his own amusement to see the arrangement of the table. There are besides several others,* which, as there are many figures in the picture, I do not recollect.

Q. What is the meaning of those men dressed in the German fashion,† each with a halbert in his hand?

A. It is now necessary that I should say a few words. ‡

The Court. Say on.

A. We painters take the same license that is permitted to poets, and jesters (!). I have placed those two halberdiers

and calls this which he represents here the last of the two, though there is nothing whatever to identify it as first, last, or middle. There is no Magdalen, no Mary, no Lazarus, no hospitable Levi, no supercilious Simon. Nothing but a confused meeting of very mixed company; half of them straggling about the table without sitting down; and the conspicuous brown dog, for whom the Inquisitors would have had him substitute the Magdalen;—which if he had done, the picture would have been right in all other particulars, the scarlet-robed figure opposite Christ then becoming Simon the Pharisee; but he cannot be Matthew the apostle, for Veronese distinctly names the twelve apostles after " the master of the house;" and the text written on the balustrade on the left is therefore either spurious altogether, or added by Veronese to get rid of the necessity of putting in a Magdalen to satisfy his examiners, or please the Prior of St. John and Paul.

* Yes, there certainly are 'several others'—some score of idlers about, I should say. But this longer answer of the painter's was probably little attended to, and ill reported by the secretary.

† My lords have suspicions of leaning towards the principles—no less than the taste—of Holbein; and of meaning some mischief.

‡ He instantly feels the drift of this last question, and that it must not be passed lightly. Asks leave to speak—(usually no license but of direct answer being given).

—the one eating, the other drinking * —by the staircase, to be supposed ready to perform any duty that may be required of them; it appearing to me quite fitting that the master of such a house, who was rich and great (as I have been told), should have such attendants.

Q. That fellow dressed like a buffoon, with the parrot on his wrist,—for what purpose is *he* introduced into the canvas?

A. For ornament, as is usually done.†

Q. At the table of the Lord whom have you placed?

A. The twelve apostles.

Q. What is St. Peter doing, who is the first? ‡

A. He is cutting up a lamb, to send to the other end of the table.

Q. What is he doing who is next to him?

A. He is holding a plate to receive what St. Peter will give him.

Q. Tell us what he is doing who is next to this last?

A. He is using a fork as a toothpick. §

Q. Who do you really think were present at that supper?

A. I believe Christ and His apostles were present; but in the foreground of the picture I have placed figures for ornament, of my own invention.

---

* On the right. *One* has got all the eating and drinking to himself, however, as far as I can see.

† Alas, *everything* is for ornament—if you would own it, Master Paul!

‡ Very curious that no question is asked as to what Christ Himself is doing. One would have greatly desired Veronese's answer.

§ Scarcely seen, between the two pillars. I must needs admit that Raphael would have invented some more dignifiedly apostolic action.

Q. Were you commissioned by any person to paint Germans, and buffoons, and such-like things in this picture?

A. No, my lord; my commission was to ornament the picture as I judged best, which, being large, requires many figures, as it appears to me.

. *Q.* Are the ornaments that the painter is in the habit of introducing in his frescoes and pictures suited and fitting to the subject and to the principal persons represented, or does he really paint such as .strike his own fancy without exercising his judgment or his discretion?*

A. I design my pictures with all due consideration as to what is fitting, and to the best of my judgment.

Q. Does it appear to you fitting that at our Lord's last supper † you should paint buffoons, drunkards, Germans,‡ dwarfs, and similar indecencies?

A. No, my lord.

Q. Why, then, have you painted them?

A. I have done it because I supposed that these were not in the place where the supper was served.

Q. Are you not aware that in Germany,§ and in other places infected with heresy, they are in the habit of painting pictures full of scurrility for the purpose of ridiculing and degrading the Holy Church, and thus teaching false doctrines to the ignorant and foolish?

A. Yes, my lord, it is bad; but I return to what I said before: I thought myself obliged to do as others—my predecessors—had done before me.

Q. And have your predecessors, then, done such things?

A. Michel-Angelo, in the Papal Chapel in Rome, has

* Admirably put, my lord.

† Not meaning the Cena, of course; but what Veronese also meant.

‡ and § The gist of the business, at last.

painted our Lord Jesus Christ, His mother, St. John, and St. Peter, and all the Court of Heaven, from the Virgin Mary downwards, all naked, and in various attitudes, with little reverence.

Q. Do you not know that in a painting like the Last Judgment, where drapery is not supposed, dresses are not required, and that disembodied spirits only are represented: but there are neither buffoons, nor dogs, nor armour, nor any other absurdity? And does it not appear to you that neither by this nor any other example you have done right in painting the picture in this manner, and that it can be proved right and decent?

A. Illustrious Lord, I do not defend it; but I thought I was doing right. I had not considered all these things, never intending to commit any impropriety; the more so as figures of buffoons are not supposed to be in the same place where our Lord is.

Which examination ended, my lords decreed that the above-named Master Paul should be bound to correct and amend the picture which had been under question, within three months, at his own expense, under penalties to be imposed by the Sacred Tribunal."

This sentence, however severe in terms, was merely a matter of form. The examiners were satisfied there was no malice prepense in their fanciful Paul; and troubled neither him nor themselves farther. He did not so much as efface the inculpated dog; and the only correction or amendment he made, so far as I can see, was the addition of the inscription which marked the picture for the feast of Levi.

Lightning Source UK Ltd.
Milton Keynes UK
26 September 2009

144208UK00006BA/2/A